Criterion-Referenced Measurement

An Introduction

Criterion-Referenced Measurement

An Introduction

•

W. James Popham
Editor

Educational Technology Publications / Englewood Cliffs, New Jersey

Library of Congress Catalog Card Number: 75-146292.

International Standard Book Number: 0-87778-006-4.

Second Printing: August, 1972.
Third Printing: April, 1973.

Foreword

Amazing progress has been made in psychological measurement since E. L. Thorndike's hopeful declaration of faith: if anything exists, it exists in quantity; and if it exists in quantity, it can be measured. An innovation, however, still has its troubles. It is at first ignored, then attacked and criticized, then perhaps tentatively accepted, incorporated in the existing system, and gradually taken for granted. The newcomers on the scene assume that it has always existed, and that it is not only desirable but necessary. This book, consisting of a series of papers—particularly the first (1963) by Robert Glaser describing one innovation—may well mark the beginning of a new era in measurement, in which case a brief summary of the development of the system in which it is seeking incorporation, as I have observed it, may not be out of place.

I was born in 1894. In that year, though I was not aware of it at the time, the 37-year-old Alfred Binet (with his collaborator, Dr. Simon) launched his attack on the psychophysical tests of Galton and others, including James McKeen Cattell in this country; and by 1905, when I reached the sixth grade, he had thirty tests of mental processes, arranged in order of difficulty in a kind of scale. In 1908, when I was ready for high school, H. H. Goddard, then director of the Vineland, New Jersey Training School for the Feeble-Minded, was using this scale in translation, and Binet had completed another revision employing the new concept of mental age. The tests were criticized as being superfluous, as "breaking down an unlocked door." It was argued that any teacher could judge the intelligence of his pupils without recourse to such a mechanical contraption. But others held a different view, like that of an English visitor who exclaimed to Binet, "It does what people have always done, but does it better!"

In 1911, the year I entered college, a final revision appeared, the year of Binet's death. And the year following my graduation, 1916, Lewis M. Terman and his colleagues at Stanford University brought out their American revised version which employed the concept of the IQ, the "mental ratio" he had borrowed from Wilhelm Stern of Hamburg.

In college I became interested in psychology through the texts of Pillsbury, James, and Angell, but had heard nothing of the others whose names have been mentioned. While teaching high school English and history, however, I got wind of a plan to test the recruits of World War I.

Having been disqualified for active military duty, I applied for admission to the training program at Camp Greenleaf, Georgia, where I made the acquaintance of Terman's *The Measurement of Intelligence,* Thorndike's *Mental and Social Measurements,* Rugg's *Statistical Methods Applied to Education,* and Whipple's *Manual of Mental and Physical Tests,* and there and in the Surgeon General's office (where I was later sent), of Yerkes, Terman, Courtis, Berry, and others in person. At camp, from John Anderson, Mark May, Carl Murchison, and others I learned more about psychological testing. And there I practiced squads right and squads left, for we were to "sell psychology" to the Army, and this required that psychologists become soldiers, or a reasonable facsimile thereof.

Through the genius of Arthur Otis, the individual tests of Binet and Terman had been translated into the group tests Army Alpha for literates and Beta for illiterates. These were administered to thousands of recruits in the several cantonments throughout the country during the hot summer of 1918, test blanks were scored by hand, and for morale purposes, among other things, as the "Singing Psychs" we gave concerts in different parts of the cantonment. One of the songs went somewhat as follows:

> Oh we'll sing, we'll sing, we'll sing of Simon Bennett
> And his tests, his tests, his tests from gay Paree,
> How he sepa-, separates the ments from the aments
> With his grand, his grand, his grand psychologee.

Psychology caught on, the idea spread, and the form was set. When the War was over, the schema of the mental test, invented to discover and predict aptitude, was remodeled for school use—not only for this purpose but also to test school achievement for diagnostic and training purposes. Standardized subject-matter tests and test batteries multiplied. The race course introduced the curve of chance, followed in short order by the correlation coefficient, age and grade norms, and courses in test and scale construction. Texts in psychology and educational psychology, measurements, and statistics spread the needed information in an increasingly competitive market. Testing became standard operating procedure, and everybody was happy.

Well, perhaps not quite everybody. It might have been all right if these new normative tests devised to differentiate and compare individuals for recommending further education and training had not got mixed up with school marks that provided false criteria, and so were mistakenly used to make decisions about individuals and instructional treatment. In any case, some worried a little about the forgotten scales of Courtis, Thorndike, and others for measuring handwriting, composition, arithmetic, etc. Some students realized that their marks in the same subject over the years did not improve, though their work was more advanced. Others were disappointed because they got, say, 69, when with one more point they would have "passed." The new letter grades (used in the Army), sometimes with plus or minus signs added, helped in this matter, but there were other strange consequences.

Some students recommended for "honors" courses declined the honor since they could not be sure of the "A" they knew they could earn in the regular course. Teachers who liked the then new objective-type, quick-scoring tests had difficulty in thinking up "distractors," i.e., wrong answers that sounded good enough to fool some of the students, and also in deciding where to make the cutting points between the letter grades, since the scores were so close together, especially in the middle of the curve.

But in general the system of letter marking on the basis of the probability curve was more under control than marks based on the per cent of answers correct. The really handy thing about it was that with the curve, what a student "got" depended on what others did. Those who got fewer answers right, it was assumed, were either stupid or hadn't done their homework; so the teacher was relieved of responsibility of teaching them very much, only for assigning letter grades and an occasional failure. Even this was too much for some; so apparently on the assumption that if little precision is good less is better, Pass-Fail marking in some places became the student's reasonably sure get-away to success.

When B. F. Skinner's programmed instruction format appeared, some diligent huntsman found a Thorndikian paragraph that described a new kind of book that would function in much the same way. I believe it would be profitable for someone to write a book with some such title as *Thorndike Revisited*. The measurement difficulties alluded to above were clearly envisioned by him as long ago as 1913. In Glaser's second article in this volume, he has included a long quotation from Thorndike's *Educational Psychology*, Vol. I, in which, among other things, he wrote:

> The detailed nature and the report to the individual of his school marks were not the vices of the old system. Its vice was its relativity and indefiniteness—the fact already described that a given mark did not mean any defined amount of knowledge, or power, or skill—so that it was bound to be used for relative achievement only. . . .
>
> Rivalry with one's own past and with a "bogey," or accepted standard, is entirely feasible, once we have absolute scales for educational achievement comparable to the scales for speed at which one can run or the height to which one can jump. Such scales are being constructed. The strength of such impersonal rivalry as a motive, while not as great for the two or three who would compete to lead the class under the old system as that system's emphasis on rivalry with others, is far greater for the rest of the group. To be seventeenth instead of eighteenth, or twenty-third instead of twenty-fifth, does not approach in moving force the zeal to beat one's own record, to see one's practice curve rise week by week, and to get up to the standard which permits one to advance to a new feat.

Note that what Thorndike referred to as "the old system" in 1913 *is the one still in use.* What are the reasons for this time lag? Granted that there are uses for scores that represent a ranking of members of a group or comparisons of individuals with such rankings, as in the use of age and grade norms and percentile or standard scores; as Glaser points out in his first (1963) article, such norm-referenced measures do not tell how proficient students are with respect to the subject-matter tasks, i.e., the objectives of instruction.

But why should such scores continue to be used for everything, whether or not they are appropriate? It would seem that absolute (criterion-referenced) scores would be used where convenient, as in track and field sports. Yet physical education teachers are required to conform to the relative pattern even though the stop watch and measuring tape provide them with absolute measures. It would seem that a person's score should be what it is, no matter what those of his age or grade may be. And further it would seem that the instruction a student receives should start with and be based on what he already knows and can do, not how much better or worse he is than someone else.

Perhaps the main reason for the lag is that World War I psychology was concerned with norm reference and so promoted this one style, while nothing equivalent to it or Sputnik has acted to generalize and motivate the use of the criterion score, though it has, of course, been used in a variety of widely separated military tasks, some of which have to be performed correctly or not at all. But this is not enough to account for the lag. A magazine editor friend of mine has opined that most top measurement men are against criterion-referenced measurement. If this is true, it would help to account for a more general lack of interest owing to the consequent slower diffusion in the absence of the prestige factor.

But if they are opposed, why should they be? Perhaps with their advanced knowledge of the field they question its possibility or practicality: they know better. Some years ago I asked one top measurement man why there was not more being done with criterion-referenced measurement. His answer was painfully direct: "We spent twenty-five years teaching the teachers about measurements, and it's too much to start all over again." Perhaps this is it—not superior knowledge but plain old apathy.

True, there are difficulties. Some are indicated in this volume, along with suggested ways of dealing with them, difficulties related to such familiar concepts as variability, reliability, validity, and item construction and analysis, as discussed by Popham and Husek, and by Cox, for example, aimed to determine whether certain course objectives such as those in social studies or even simple addition have been met. The question of when to use one or the other form of testing is worked over by Garvin, and that of the adequacy of criterion-referenced items in determining the degree of mastery of content objectives by Popham. As to the apathy and inertia, possibly the solution is to set student activist groups on the trail of the measurement people with a "demand" for criterion measures!

In any case, many will be delighted to find Glaser's heretofore rather elusive term conveniently located in the title of a book, and a small book at that, but authored by experts and ranging in content from basic concepts to reports of statistical studies, and containing a goodly list of references.

Not the least advantage to be gained from wider appreciation of the nature of NRM and CRM, like the development of programmed instruction, is that it should tend to bring educational objectives out into the open to be shot at and perhaps eventually tamed.

Wm. Clark Trow
Professor Emeritus of Education and Psychology
The University of Michigan

Preface

At the 1970 meeting of the American Educational Research Association in Minneapolis a symposium was presented on the topic, *Criterion-Referenced Measurement: Emerging Issues*. That the symposium, jointly sponsored by the National Council on Measurement in Education, attracted a large audience was not surprising—many educators, particularly educational researchers, have now recognized the necessity for newer approaches to measuring the results of instruction. What was surprising, at least to some of us, was the high level of technical discourse which occurred during the post-presentations discussion period. It was apparent that measurement specialists were beginning to direct their talents toward the solution of the numerous problems faced by those wishing to employ more recent approaches to measurement, and this was new. Since Robert Glaser's classic 1963 article in the *American Psychologist* calling for altered approaches to the measurement of learning outcomes, there has been a fair amount of talk, but little productive progress in providing the technical constructs and techniques needed to develop high quality criterion-referenced measures. We have often heard why certain types of time-honored measurement ploys are not appropriate for criterion-referenced measures. Few alternatives, however, have been proposed. The symposium in question was designed to stimulate activity along these lines. Appropriately enough, the symposium was chaired by Robert Glaser, whose periodic comments and writing since the 1963 paper have done much to stimulate interest on this topic.

We were delighted when the publishers of this volume, upon examining copies of the symposium papers, proposed that a brief book be assembled, for this would represent one additional way of getting colleagues to tackle the tricky technical problems facing us all.

In consultation with Professor Glaser and the publishers it seemed wise to precede the symposium papers with three introductory articles which prove useful, particularly for the reader who has not encountered the basic distinctions involved. We commence with the 1963 Glaser article, followed by a more recent paper by the late T. R. Husek and myself. A third paper, by Glaser, is based on a chapter he recently co-authored with Anthony J. Nitko ("Measurement in Learning and Instruction" to appear in *Educational Measurement,* R. L. Thorndike, Editor). Whereas the earlier paper by Glaser essentially expressed his puzzlement and some thoughts designed to stimulate others, his recent writing provides us with a better definition of a criterion-referenced test.

Following these three introductory papers, the symposium papers are then presented in the order they were given in Minneapolis by Professors Alfred D. Garvin, Richard C. Cox and myself.

W. James Popham
University of California, Los Angeles

Contents

xvii

Criterion-Referenced Measurement

An Introduction

Instructional Technology and the Measurement of Learning Outcomes
SOME QUESTIONS

Instructional Technology and the Measurement of Learning Outcomes
SOME QUESTIONS*

Robert Glaser

University of Pittsburgh

Evaluation of the effectiveness of teaching machines and programed learning, and of broadly conceived instructional systems, has raised into prominence a number of questions concerning the nature and properties of measures of student achievement. In the evaluation of instructional systems, the attainment of subject matter

---

*Reprinted from *American Psychologist,* 1963, *18,* 519-521. Copyright © 1963 by the American Psychological Association, and reproduced by permission.

knowledge and skill as well as other behavioral outcomes must, of course, be considered, but the remarks in this paper will be restricted primarily to the measurement of subject matter proficiency, as it may be defined by recognized subject matter scholars.

Achievement measurement can be defined as the assessment of terminal or criterion behavior; this involves the determination of the characteristics of student performance with respect to specified standards. Achievement measurement is distinguished from aptitude measurement in that the instruments used to assess achievement are specifically concerned with the characteristics and properties of present performance, with emphasis on the meaningfulness of its content. In contrast, aptitude measures derive their meaning from a demonstrated relationship between present performance and the future attainment of specified knowledge and skill. In certain circumstances, of course, this contrast is not quite so clear, for example, when achievement measures are used as predictor variables.

The scores obtained from an achievement test provide primarily two kinds of information. One is the degree to which the student has attained criterion performance,

---

This paper is from a symposium address presented at the American Educational Research Association, Chicago, February 1963. The paper is concerned with student educational achievement; however, similar notions have been expressed with respect to the human component in man-machine systems in R. Glaser and D. J. Klaus (1962).

for example, whether he can satisfactorily prepare an experimental report, or solve certain kinds of word problems in arithmetic. The second type of information that an achievement test score provides is the relative ordering of individuals with respect to their test performance, for example, whether Student A can solve his problems more quickly than Student B. The principal difference between these two kinds of information lies in the standard used as a reference. What I shall call criterion-referenced measures depend upon an absolute standard of quality, while what I term norm-referenced measures depend upon a relative standard. Distinctions between these two kinds of measures have been made previously by others (Flanagan, 1951; Ebel, 1962).

Criterion-Referenced Measures

Underlying the concept of achievement measurement is the notion of a continuum of knowledge acquisition ranging from no proficiency at all to perfect performance. An individual's achievement level falls at some point on this continuum as indicated by the behaviors he displays during testing. The degree to which his achievement resembles desired performance at any specified level is assessed by criterion-referenced measures of achievement or proficiency. The standard against which a student's performance is compared when measured in this manner is the behavior which defines each point along the achievement continuum. The term "criterion," when used in this

way, does not necessarily refer to final end-of-course behavior. Criterion levels can be established at any point in
instruction where it is necessary to obtain information as
to the adequacy of an individual's performance. The
point is that the specific behaviors implied at each level
of proficiency can be identified and used to describe the
specific tasks a student must be capable of performing
before he achieves one of these knowledge levels. It is in
this sense that measures of proficiency can be criterion-
referenced.

Along such a continuum of attainment, a student's
score on a criterion-referenced measure provides explicit
information as to what the individual can or cannot do.
Criterion-referenced measures indicate the content of the
behavioral repertory, and the correspondence between
what an individual does and the underlying continuum
of achievement. Measures which assess student achievement in terms of a criterion standard thus provide information as to the degree of competence attained by a
particular student which is independent of reference to
the performance of others.

Norm-Referenced Measures

On the other hand, achievement measures also convey
information about the capability of a student compared
with the capability of other students. In instances where
a student's *relative* standing along the continuum of attainment is the primary purpose of measurement, ref-

erence need not be made to criterion behavior. Educational achievement examinations, for example, are administered frequently for the purpose of ordering students in a class or school, rather than for assessing their attainment of specified curriculum objectives. When such norm-referenced measures are used, a particular student's achievement is evaluated in terms of a comparison between his performance and the performance of other members of the group. Such measures need provide little or no information about the degree of proficiency exhibited by the tested behaviors in terms of what the individual can do. They tell that one student is more or less proficient than another, but do not tell how proficient either of them is with respect to the subject matter tasks involved.

In large part, achievement measures currently employed in education are norm-referenced. This emphasis upon norm-referenced measures has been brought about by the preoccupation of test theory with aptitude,. and with selection and prediction problems; norm-referenced measures are useful for this kind of work in correlational analysis. However, the imposition of this kind of thinking on the purposes of achievement measurement raises some question, and concern with instructional technology is forcing us toward the kind of information made available by the use of criterion-referenced measures. We need to behaviorally specify minimum levels of performance that describe the least amount of end-of-course competence the student is expected to attain, or that he needs in order to go on to the next course in a sequence. The specification of the characteristics of maximum or optimum achievement after a student has been exposed to the course of instruction poses more difficult problems of criterion delineation.

The Uses of Achievement Measurement

Consider a further point. In the context of the evaluation of instructional systems, achievement tests can be used for two principal purposes. First, performance can be assessed to provide information about the characteristics of an individual's present behavior. Second, achievement can be assessed to provide information about the conditions or instructional treatments which produce that behavior. The primary emphasis of the first use is to discriminate among individuals. Used in the second way, achievement tests are employed to discriminate among treatments, that is, among different instructional procedures by an analysis of *group* differences.

Achievement tests used to provide information about *individual* differences are constructed so as to maximize the discriminations made among people having specified backgrounds and experience. Such tests include items which maximize the likelihood of observing individual differences in performance along various task dimensions; this maximizes the variability of the distribution of scores that are obtained. In practical test construction, the variability of test scores is increased by manipulating the difficulty levels and content of the test items.

On the other hand, achievement tests used primarily to provide information about differences in treatments need to be constructed so as to maximize the discriminations made between *groups* treated differently and to minimize the differences between the individuals in any one group. Such a test will be sensitive to the differences produced by instructional conditions. For example, a test designed to demonstrate the effectiveness of instruction would be constructed so that it was generally difficult for those taking it before training and generally easy after training. The content of the test used to differentiate treatments should be maximally sensitive to the performance changes anticipated from the instructional treatments. In essence, the distinction between achievement tests used to maximize individual differences and tests used to maximize treatment or group differences is established during the selection of test items.

In constructing an achievement test to differentiate among *individuals* at the end of training, it would be possible to begin by obtaining data on a large sample of items relating to curriculum objectives. Item analysis would indicate that some test items were responded to correctly only by some of the individuals in the group, while other items were answered correctly by all members of the group. These latter 1.00 difficulty level items, since they failed to differentiate among individuals, would be eliminated because their only effect would be to add a constant to every score. The items remaining would serve to discriminate among individuals and thus yield a distribution of scores that was as large as possible, considering the number and type of items used.

On the other hand, if this test were constructed for the purpose of observing *group* instead of individual differences, the selection of items would follow a different course. For example, where instruction was the treatment variable involved, it would be desirable to retain test items which were responded to correctly by all members of the post-training group, but which were answered incorrectly by students who had not yet been trained. In a test constructed for the purpose of differentiating groups, items which indicated substantial variability within either the pre- or post-training group would be undesirable because of the likelihood that they would cloud the effects which might be attributable to the treatment variable.

In brief, items most suitable for measuring individual differences in achievement are those which will differentiate among individuals all exposed to the same treatment variable, while items most suitable for distinguishing between groups are those which are most likely to indicate that a given amount or kind of some instructional treatment was effective. In either case, samples of test items are drawn from a population of items indicating the content of performance; the particular item samples that are drawn, however, are those most useful for the purpose of the kind of measurement being carried out. Hammock (1960) has previously discussed such a difference.

The points indicated above reflect the achievement measurement concerns that have arisen in my own work with instructional technology. There is one further point which must be mentioned, and that is the use of diagnostic achievement tests prior to an instructional course. It appears that, with the necessity for specifying the entering behavior that is required by a student prior to a programed instructional sequence, diagnostic assessment of subject matter competence must take on a more precise function. This raises the problem of developing an improved methodology for diagnostic achievement testing. In this regard, researchers using programed instructional sequences to study learning variables point out that prior testing influences learning, and that this effect must be controlled for in determining the specific contribution of programing variables. In an instructional sense, however, the influence and use of pretesting is an important variable for study since it is not the terminal criterion behavior alone which dictates required instructional manipulations, but the differences between entering and terminal behavior. Furthermore, pretesting of a special kind may contribute to "motivation" by enhancing the value of future responses; there is some indication that this may be brought about by prior familiarity with future response terms (Berlyne, 1960, pp. 296-301) or by permitting some early aided performance of the terminal behavior eventually to be engaged in (Taber, Glaser, & Schaefer, 1963, Ch. 3).

In conclusion, the general point is this: Test development has been dominated by the particular requirements of predictive, correlational aptitude test "theory." Achievement and criterion measurement has attempted frequently to cast itself in this framework. However, many of us are beginning to recognize that the problems of assessing existing levels of competence and achievement and the conditions that produce them require some additional considerations.

References

Berlyne, D. E. *Conflict, arousal, and curiosity.* New York: McGraw-Hill, 1960.

Ebel, R. L. Content standard test scores. *Educ. Psychol. Measmt.*, 1962, *22*, 15-25.

Flanagan, J. C. Units, scores, and norms. In E. T. Lindquist (Ed.), *Educational measurement.* Washington, D. C.: American Council on Education, 1951. Pp. 695-763.

Glaser, R., & Klaus, D. J. Proficiency measurement: Assessing human performance. In R. Gagné (Ed.), *Psychological principles in system development.* New York: Holt, Rinehart & Winston, 1962. Pp. 421-427.

Hammock, J. Criterion measures: Instruction vs. selection research. *Amer. Psychologist,* 1960, *15*, 435. (Abstract)

Taber, J. I., Glaser, R., & Schaefer, H. H. *A guide to the preparation of programmed instructional materials.* Reading, Mass.: Addison-Wesley, 1963.

Implications of
Criterion-Referenced
Measurement

Implications of Criterion-Referenced Measurement*

W. James Popham
University of California, Los Angeles
and
T. R. Husek
University of California, Los Angeles

During the past several years measurement and instructional specialists have distinguished between *norm-referenced* and *criterion-referenced* approaches to measurement. More traditional, a norm-referenced measure is used to identify an individual's performance in relation to the performance of others on the same measure. A criterion-referenced test is used to identify

*Reprinted by permission from the *Journal of Educational Measurement,* 1969, 6 (1), 1-9.

an individual's status with respect to an established standard of performance. This discussion examines the implications of these two approaches to measurement, particularly criterion-referenced measurement, with respect to variability, item construction, reliability, validity, item analysis, reporting, and interpretation.

The question of what score to use as the most meaningful index of a student's performance on a test has been the subject of many discussions over the years. Percentile scores, raw scores, and standard scores of various kinds have been advocated. The arguments have almost always begun with the premise that the test is a given and that the issue is how to obtain the meaningful score. That is, there has been general acceptance of how the test should be constructed and judged. Test theory as explicated in most elementary testing texts has been assumed to represent a commonly held set of values. In recent years some writers (e. g., Cronbach and Gleser, 1965) have begun to question the usefulness of classical test theory for all testing problems. This broadens and complicates the question above; the problem is now not only how to summarize a student's performance on a test, but also how to insure that a test is constructed (and judged) in a manner appropriate to its use, even if its use is not in the classical framework.

One facet of this issue has particular relevance to tests based on instructional objectives. For several years now, particularly since the appearance of Glaser's article

(1963) on the subject, measurement and instructional specialists have been drawing distinctions between so-called *norm-referenced* and *criterion-referenced* approaches to measurement. But it appears that, other than adding new terms to the technical lexicon, the two constructs have made little difference in measurement practice. Perhaps the reason for this is that few analyses have been made of the practical implications of using criterion-referenced measures. Most of us are familiar with concepts associated with norm-referenced measurement. We grew up with them. A criterion-referenced approach, however, is another matter. What differences, if any, does a criterion-referenced framework make with respect to such operations as test construction and revision, and to such concepts as reliability and validity? This article will examine some of these implications by contrasting criterion-referenced and norm-referenced approaches with respect to such central measurement notions.

The Basic Distinction

It is not possible to tell a *norm-referenced* test from a *criterion-referenced* test by looking at it. In fact a *criterion-referenced* test could also be used as a *norm-referenced* test—although the reverse is not so easy to imagine. However, this truth should not be allowed to obscure the extremely important differences between these two approaches to testing.

At the most elementary level, norm-referenced measures are those which are used to ascertain an individual's performance in relationship to the performance of other individuals on the same measuring device. The meaningfulness of the individual score emerges from the comparison. It is because the individual is compared with some normative group that such measures are described as norm-referenced. Most standardized tests of achievement or intellectual ability can be classified as norm-referenced measures.

Criterion-referenced measures are those which are used to ascertain an individual's status with respect to some criterion, i. e., performance standard. It is because the individual is compared with some established criterion, rather than other individuals, that these measures are described as criterion-referenced. The meaningfulness of an individual score is not dependent on comparison with other testees. We want to know what the individual can do, not how he stands in comparison to others. For example, the dog owner who wants to keep his dog in the back yard may give his dog a fence-jumping test. The owner wants to find out how high the dog can jump so that the owner can build a fence high enough to keep the dog in the yard. How the dog compares with other dogs is irrelevant. Another example of a criterion-referenced test would be the Red Cross Senior Lifesaving Test, where an individual must display certain swimming skills to pass the examination irrespective of how well others perform on the test.

Since norm-referenced measures are devised to facilitate comparisons among individuals, it is not surprising that their primary purpose is to make decisions about *individuals*. Which pupil should be counseled to pursue higher education? Which pupils should be advised to attain vocational skills? These are the kinds of questions one seeks to answer through the use of norm-referenced measures, for many decisions regarding an individual can best be made by knowing more about the "competition," that is, by knowing how other, comparable individuals perform.

Criterion-referenced tests are devised to make decisions both about *individuals and treatments,* e. g., instructional programs. In the case of decisions regarding individuals, one might use a criterion-referenced test to determine whether a learner had mastered a criterion skill considered prerequisite to his commencing a new training program. In the case of decisions regarding treatments, one might design a criterion-referenced measure which reflected a set of instructional objectives supposedly achieved by a replicable instructional sequence. By administering the criterion-referenced measure to appropriate learners after they had completed the instructional sequence, one could reach a decision regarding the efficacy of the sequence (treatment).

Although both norm-referenced and criterion-referenced tests are used to make decisions about individuals, there is usually a difference in the two contexts in which such decisions are made. Generally, a norm-referenced measure is employed where a degree of *selectivity* is required by the situation. For example, when there are only limited openings in a company's executive training program, the company is anxious to identify the *best* potential trainees. It is critical in such situations, therefore, that the measure permit *relative* comparisons among individuals. On the other hand, in situations where one is only interested in whether an individual possesses a particular competence, and there are no constraints regarding how many individuals can possess that skill, criterion-referenced measures are suitable. Theoretically, at the close of many instructional programs we might hope that *all* learners would display *maximum* proficiency on measures reflecting the instructional objectives. In this sense, of course, criterion-referenced measures may be considered *absolute* indicators. Thus, both norm-referenced and criterion-referenced tests can be focused on decisions regarding individuals—it is the context within which these decisions are made that really produces the distinction.

Now one could, of course, use norm-referenced measures as well as criterion-referenced measures to make decisions regarding the merits of instructional programs. Certainly, this has been a common practice through the years as educators have evaluated their curriculum efforts on the basis of pupil performance on standardized examinations. But norm-referenced measures were really designed to "spread people out" and, as we shall see, are best suited to that purpose.

With this initial distinction in mind, we shall now examine the implications of the two approaches to measurement, particularly with respect to criterion-referenced measures, for the following topics: variability, item construction, reliability, validity, item analysis, reporting, and interpretation.

Variability

The issue of variability is at the core of the difference between norm-referenced and criterion-referenced tests. Since the meaningfulness of a norm-referenced score is basically dependent on the relative position of the score in comparison with other scores, the more variability in the scores the better. With a norm-referenced test, we want to be able to tell Jamie from Joey from Frank, and we feel more secure about telling them apart if their scores are very different.

With criterion-referenced tests, variability is irrelevant. The meaning of the score is not dependent on comparison with other scores; it flows directly from the connection between the items and the criterion. It is, of course, true that one almost always gets variant scores on any psychological test; but that variability is not a necessary condition for a good criterion-referenced test.

The subtle and not-so-subtle implications of this central difference in the relevance of variability must permeate any discussion of the two approaches to testing. For example, we all have been told that a test should be reliable and valid. We have all read about test construction and item analysis. The procedures may not always be simple, the formulas may not be trivial; but there are hundreds of books and thousands of articles to guide us. Unfortunately, most of what these "helpmates" outline as "good" things to do are not only irrelevant to criterion-referenced tests, but are actually injurious to their proper development and use. This is true because the treatments of validity, the suggestions about reliability, and the formulas for item analysis are all based on the desirability of variability among scores. The connection may not be obvious but it is always there.

Item Construction

The basic difference between item construction in norm-referenced and criterion-referenced frameworks is a matter of "set" on the part of the item writer. Until we reach that automated era when computers can cough forth many items per minute, someone is going to have to construct them. The primary differences in purposes of norm-referenced and criterion-referenced measurement will usually influence the item writer to a considerable degree in at least one very significant way and, possibly to a lesser extent, in a second way as well.

Most important, when a writer constructs items for a norm-referenced test, he wants variability and, as a consequence, makes all sorts of concessions, sometimes subtle, sometimes obvious, to promote variant scores. He disdains items which are "too easy" or "too hard." He tries to increase the allure of wrong answer options. All of this he does to produce variability. Occasionally this overriding criterion may reduce the adequacy of the instrument, for even spurious factors may be incorporated in items just to produce variance.

The criterion-referenced item writer is guided by another goal. His chief rule is to make sure the item is an accurate reflection of the criterion behavior. Difficult or easy, discriminating or indiscriminate, the important thing is to make the item represent the class of behaviors delimited by the criterion. Those who write criterion-referenced items are usually far more attentive to defining the domain of relevant test responses and the situations in which they should be required. This rather fundamental difference in "set" on the part of criterion-referenced and norm-referenced item writers can clearly contribute to differences in the resulting items.

A second difference associated with test construction is that although norm-referenced and criterion-referenced measures which are used to make decisions regarding individuals require that the same test (or an equivalent form) be used with different individuals, criterion-referenced tests used for evaluating programs need not. The concept of item sampling (Cronbach, 1963; Husek and Sirotnik, 1968) in which different people complete different items (thereby permitting the sampling of more behavior with shorter tests) is highly appropriate for evaluating the adequacy of treatments. Thus, for such situations a number of different test forms, each containing different criterion-referenced items, could be constructed. Individuals nurtured on the concept of "everybody gets the same items" will often overlook this economic, yet powerful shortcut.

Once the test is originally devised, we would like to have procedures available for improving it. In a norm-referenced context we have available the time-honored devices such as item analysis techniques and reliability estimates which can guide us in test refinement operations. With criterion-referenced measures, however, some of these classical constructs must be used differently. The next few sections of this paper will describe the nature of these differences.

Reliability

We all should know that for a single number to be used to describe the performance of a person on a test, the items on that test should all "measure the same thing" to some minimal extent. That is, the test should be internally consistent. This matter is treated in measurement texts in the chapter on reliability.

Now it is obvious that a criterion-referenced test should be internally consistent. If we argue that the items are tied to a criterion, then certainly the items should be quite similar in terms of what they are measuring. But although it may be obvious that a criterion-referenced test should be internally consistent, it is not obvious how to assess the internal consistency. The classical procedures are not appropriate. This is true because they are dependent on score variability. A criterion-referenced test should not be faulted if, when administered after instruction, everyone obtained a perfect score. Yet, that would lead to a zero internal consistency estimate, something measurement books don't recommend.

In fact, even stranger things can happen in practice. It is possible for a criterion-referenced test to have a *negative* internal consistency index and still be a good test. (See Husek and Sirotnik, 1968, for a more extensive treatment of this possibility.)

Thus, the typical indices of internal consistency are not appropriate for criterion-referenced tests. It is not clear what should replace them. Perhaps we need estimates, comparable to the standard internal consistency formulas, which can take larger temporal units into consideration, for example, by considering both a pre-instruction test administration and a post-instruction test administration as part of the same extended phenomenon. Perhaps ingenious indices can be developed which reflect the ability of a test to produce variation from pre-instruction to post-instruction testing and, in these terms, internal consistency—despite score range restrictions. But until that time, those wishing to improve criterion-referenced tests should not be dismayed if the test, because of little score variance, yields a low internal consistency estimate. It is really unwise to apply such estimates.

The foregoing discussion applies only to situations where the test is used to assess a single dimension, such as one instructional objective, as opposed to several dimensions, such as three very disparate objectives. If the objectives are substantially different, the items measuring them should be considered as different tests, not a single all-encompassing measure.

Other aspects of reliability are equally cloudy. Stability might certainly be important for a criterion-referenced test, but in that case, a test-retest correlation coefficient, dependent as it is on variability, is not necessarily the way to assess it. Some kind of confidence interval around the individual score is perhaps a partial solution to this problem.

The reader should not misinterpret the above statements. If a criterion-referenced test has a high average inter-item correlation, this is fine. If the test has a high test-retest correlation, that is also fine. The point is *not* that these indices cannot be used to support the consistency of the test. The point is that a criterion-referenced test could be highly consistent, either internally or temporally, and yet indices dependent on variability might not reflect that consistency.

Validity

Many of the procedures for assessing the validity of

norm-referenced tests are based on correlations and thus on variability. Hence, with validity, as with reliability, the results of the procedures are useful if they are positive, but not necessarily devastating if they are negative.

Criterion-referenced measures are validated primarily in terms of the adequacy with which they represent the criterion. Therefore, content validity approaches are more suited to such tests. A carefully made judgment, based on the test's apparent relevance to the behaviors legitimately inferable from those delimited by the criterion, is the general procedure for validating criterion-referenced measures.

Certainly, for both norm-referenced and criterion-referenced measures a test specialist might employ construct validity strategies to support the confidence he can give to his instruments. For example, we might wish to augment our confidence in a measure we were using as a proximate predictor (e. g., administered at the close of instruction) of some more distant criterion (e. g., occurring many years hence). If positive intercorrelations occur among several proximate predictors (of the same distant criterion), we could add to our understanding of whether a given proximate predictor was doing its job.

Item Analysis

Item analysis procedures have traditionally been used with norm-referenced tests to identify those items that were not properly discriminating among individuals taking the test. For instance, in an achievement test an unsatisfactory item would be one which could not properly discriminate between the more and less knowledgeable learners (as reflected by total test performance). Non-discriminating items are usually those which are (a) too easy, (b) too hard, and/or (c) ambiguous.

For criterion-referenced tests the use of discrimination indices must be modified. An item which doesn't discriminate need not be eliminated. If it reflects an important attribute of the criterion, such an item should remain in the test. We might be interested in a "non-discriminating" item's ability to discriminate among *anyone*, e. g., its ability to discriminate between those individuals who have and those who haven't been exposed to instruction. But, just as in the case of reliability estimates, such indices are not currently available.

A positively discriminating item is just as respectable in a criterion-referenced test as it is in a norm-referenced test, but certainly not more so. In fact, the positively discriminating item may point to areas of instruction (if the criterion measure is assessing the effects of instruction) where the program is not succeeding well enough.

However, negatively discriminating items are treated exactly the same way in a criterion-referenced approach as they are in a norm-referenced approach. An item which discriminates negatively is one which, in an instructional context, is answered correctly more often by the less knowledgeable than by the more knowledgeable students. When one discovers a negative discriminator in his pool of criterion-referenced items, he should be suspicious of it and after more careful analysis can usually detect flaws in such an item.

Of course, discrimination indices are little more than warning flags, and one must still use common sense in weighing the worth of an item identified as a negative discriminator. It might be that some deficiencies in the instruction caused the result rather than any fault of the item. Yet, it is more likely that the item is deficient. For example, suppose that the negatively discriminating item was originally generated, along with 19 other items, as a measure of a particular type of criterion behavior. Now in order for the item to yield a negative discrimination index there would first have to be variable subject performance. But in addition, more of those individuals who scored well on the total 20-item test would have to miss the suspect item more frequently than those who scored badly on the total test. Under such circumstances it seems more likely that it is an item deficiency, rather than instructional deficiency, although the latter possibility should be kept in mind.

Is it worth the trouble? Since we are only concerned with the identification of negative discriminators, not non-discriminators, should criterion-referenced measures be subjected to item analysis operations? This would seem to depend on the ease with which one can conduct the necessary analyses. As data-processing becomes increasingly automated and less expensive, such analyses would seem warranted in situations where the effort is not immense.

Reporting and Interpretation

We use norm-referenced and criterion-referenced tests to make decisions about both individuals and treatments. We need, therefore, to interpret test results properly in order to make the best possible decisions. With respect to norm-referenced measurement the methods of interpreting the results of an individual's test performance are well known. Since we are interested in an individual's performance with respect to the performance of other individuals, we use such group-relative descriptors as percentile rankings or standard scores. Such indices allow us to tell, from a single score, how well the individual performed in relationship to the group.

When interpreting an individual's performance on a criterion-referenced test, however, such group-relative indices are not appropriate. Some criterion-referenced tests yield scores which are essentially "on-off" in nature, that is, the individual has either mastered the criterion or he hasn't. For example, certain examinations in the chemistry laboratory may require a pupil to combine and treat chemical compounds in such a way that they produce hydrogen. In such tests it is sufficient to report whether or not the learner has displayed the desired criterion behavior.

More commonly, however, a range of acceptable performances exists. For example, suppose that an instructional objective had been devised which required a learner to multiply correctly pairs of three-digit numbers. We could prepare 20 items composed of randomly selected digits to measure this skill. Because of possible computation errors, the required proficiency level for each successful student might be set at 90 per cent, or better, thereby allowing errors on two of the 20 items. In reporting an individual's performance on a test such as this, one alternative is to once more use an "on-off" approach, namely, either the 90 per cent minimum has been achieved or it hasn't.

Whether we wish to report the degree of less-than criterion performance should depend *exclusively* on the use we can make of the data. For example, if there are only two courses of action available to the individual, depending on his success or failure with respect to the criterion, then we need only report it as that, success or failure. However, if some differential experiences are to be provided on the basis of the degree of his less-than-criterion performance, then one would be interested in how far away he was from the criterion. For instance, if there were two remedial multiplication programs available, one for those very close to criterion and one for those who scored 60 per cent or below on the 20-item examination, then we would report the degree of his performance. The point is that such gradations in reporting are only a function of the alternative courses of action available to the individual after the measurement has been made.

With respect to the evaluation of treatments, it has already been pointed out that norm-referenced measures are not the most suitable devices for such purposes since their emphasis on producing heterogeneous performance sometimes diverts them from adequately reflecting the treatment's intended objectives. In using criterion-referenced measures for purposes of treatment assessment, e. g., testing the merits of a new set of programmed mathematics materials, we have several alternatives. We could simply report the number of individuals who achieve the pre-established criterion. Although such a procedure seems to supply scant data, it has the advantage of making graphically clear the proportion of learners who did not achieve criterion level proficiency. Too often this result is masked through the use of statistical averages.

We could also use traditional descriptive statistics such as means and standard deviations. Because one is often interested in the average performance produced by a treatment, as well as its variability, such statistics are useful. An average "percentage correct," however, is a helpful addition. Sometimes, if the criterion level for an individual has been set at a particular level, it is useful to report the proportion of the group which reached that level. For instance, using 80 per cent as a criterion level, then one might describe a group's performance as 92-80, indicating that 92 per cent of the group had achieved 80 per cent or better on the test. Such reporting, however, overlooks the proportion and degree of the better-than-criterion performance. It would seem, then, that in using criterion-referenced measures to make decisions about treatments, the best course of action would be to employ a number of these schemes to report the group's performance in order to permit more enlightened interpretations.

Different Kinds of Criterion-Referenced Tests

Up to this point we have discussed criterion-referenced tests as if there were one such animal. Actually, there are two. One could be said to be the ideal case and the other the more typical case.

In the ideal case the items are not only tied to the criterion but, in addition, the test is homogeneous in a very special sense. Everyone who gets the same score on the test has obtained the score in essentially the same manner. The meaning of a score is thus altogether unambiguous. If we know a person's score we know his response pattern; we know within error limits exactly what he can and cannot do. This would be an ideal criterion-referenced test, since it not only eliminates the need for a reference group but also immediately tells us the behavior repertoire of the student for that criterion. This kind of test has been discussed in the literature for some time. Guttman mentioned it as early as 1944 and Tucker elaborated on the concept in 1952.

Unfortunately, this kind of test is still mostly a dream

for educational testers. Since we need to know an immense amount about the subject matter of the test, and perhaps even about the reasons why students make certain kinds of responses, these tests at the present time are found only in relatively restricted and formal areas such as mathematics.

The other type of criterion-referenced test is more typical. The items on the test can be thought of as a sample from a potentially large group that might be generated from a criterion. The score on the test is not completely unambiguous; if we know that a student earned a score of 90 per cent correct, we do not know which items he missed. However, we do know, if we have constructed our test properly, that of the items defining the criterion behavior the student missed only 10 per cent. And if the test is homogeneous, this tells us a great deal about what the student can do.

The purpose of the foregoing discussion has been to draw distinctions between norm-referenced and criterion-referenced measurement with respect to several key measurement constructs. Because of the recency of its introduction into the field, criterion-referenced measurement received most attention. This should not imply any superiority of one approach over the other. Each has its relatively distinct role to play. The roles are only relatively distinct because one can usually employ a test developed for one purpose in another situation and still derive useful information from it. It seems, however, that there are some psychometric properties of these two types of measurement which render them most appropriate for the purposes for which they were originally designed.

References

Cronbach, L. J. Evaluation for course improvement. *Teachers College Record,* 1963, *64,* 672-683.

Cronbach, L. J. & Gleser, G. C. *Psychological tests and personnel decisions.* (2nd ed.) Urbana: University of Illinois Press, 1965.

Glaser, R. Instructional technology and the measurement of learning outcomes: Some questions. *American Psychologist,* 1963, *18,* 519-521.

Guttman, L. A basis for scaling qualitative ideas. *American Sociological Review,* 1944, *9,* 139-150.

Husek, T. R. & Sirotnik, K. Item sampling in educational research: An empirical investigation. Paper presented at the national meeting of the American Educational Research Association, Chicago, February 1968. Available as NAPS Document 00255 from ASIS National Auxiliary Publications Service, c/o CCM Information Sciences, Inc., 22 West 34th Street, New York City 10001. Remit $1.00 for microfiche or $3.00 for photocopies.

Lord, F. M. & Novick, M. R. *Statistical theories of mental test scores.* Reading, Massachusetts: Addison-Wesley, 1968.

Tucker, L. Scales minimizing the importance of reference groups. In *Proceedings, invitational conference on testing problems.* Princeton, New Jersey: Educational Testing Service, 1952. Pp. 22-28.

A Criterion-Referenced Test

A Criterion-Referenced Test

Robert Glaser

University of Pittsburgh

A criterion-referenced test is one that is deliberately constructed to yield measurements that are directly interpretable in terms of specified performance standards. Performance standards are generally specified by defining a class or domain of tasks that should be performed by the individual. Measurements are taken on representative samples of tasks drawn from this domain and such measurements are referenced directly to this domain for each individual measured.

Criterion-referenced tests are not designed only to facilitate individual difference comparisons such as the relative standing of an examinee in a norm group or population, nor are they designed to facilitate interpretations about an examinee's relative standing with respect to a hypothetical variable such as reading ability. Rather,

they are specifically constructed to support generalizations about an individual's performance relative to a
specified domain of tasks.

When the term "criterion-referenced test" is used, it
has a somewhat different meaning from the two more
prevalent uses of the terms criterion or criterion tests in
educational and psychological measurement literature.
One of these usages involves the notion that scores on
an achievement measuring instrument (X) correlate with
scores derived from a second measurement situation (Y),
this second situation being, for example, scores on another
achievement test or performance ratings such as grades.
With this usage, the Y-scores are often termed criterion
scores and the degree to which the achievement test ap-
proximates, or relates to, the criterion is often expressed
by the product-moment correlation, r_{xy}. Since the achievement test scores have the potential for correlating with
a variety of other measures, relationships to multiple
criteria are often reported. A second prevalent interpretation of the term criterion in achievement measurement
concerns the imposition of an acceptable score magnitude
as an index of attainment. The phrases "working to criterion level" and "mastery is indicated by obtaining a
score equivalent to 80 per cent of the items correct" are
indicative of this type of interpretation of criterion. Often
both of these uses of the term criterion are applied to a
single measuring instrument: A test may serve to define

the criterion to be measured, and students may be selected according to some cut-off score on it.

In the preceding chapter, Popham and Husek indicate that the distinction between a norm-referenced test and a criterion-referenced test is not easily made by the inspection of a particular instrument. The distinction is found by examining (a) the purpose for which the test was constructed, (b) the manner in which it was constructed, (c) the specificity of the information yielded about the domain of instructionally relevant tasks, (d) the generalizability of test performance information to the domain, and (e) the use to be made of the obtained test information.

Since criterion-referenced tests are specifically designed to provide information that is directly interpretable in terms of specified performance standards, this means that performance standards must be established prior to test construction and that the purpose of testing is to assess an individual's status with respect to these standards. Tests constructed for this purpose yield measurements for an individual that can be interpreted without referencing these measurements to other individuals, i.e., a norm-group. This distinction is a key one in determining whether or not a test is criterion-referenced or norm-referenced.

One source of confusion between the type of test discussed here and the typical achievement test of traditional usage resides in the notion of defining task domains and sampling from them in order to obtain test items. Arguments are often put forth that any achievement test defines a criterion in the sense that it is representative of desired outcomes and that one can determine the particular skills an individual can perform by simply examining his responses to the items on the test. The problem is, of course, that in practice desired outcomes have seldom been specified in performance terms prior to test construction. Further, the items that finally appear on a test have typically been subject to a rather rigorous sifting procedure designed to maximize the test constructor's conception of what the final distribution of test scores should be like and how the items of the test should function statistically. Ease of administration and scoring are often other determinants of what the final test task will be. Test construction practices often lead to tests comprised of tasks that tend to distort interpretations about the capabilities of the examinee with respect to a clearly defined domain of performance standards.

The distinction between norm-referenced and criterion-referenced tests can often be determined by examining the specificity of the information that can be obtained by the test in relation to the domain of relevant tasks. Logical transition from the test to the domain and back again from the domain should be readily accomplished for criterion-referenced tests, so that there is little difficulty in identifying with some degree of confidence the class of tasks that can be performed. This means that the task domain measured by criterion-referenced tests must be defined in terms of observable behavior and that the test is a representative sample of the performance domain from which competence is inferred.

Thus, the attainment of "reading ability" can only be inferred to have occurred. The basis for this inference is observable performance on the specified domain of tasks into which "reading ability" has been analyzed, such as, reading aloud, identifying an object described in a text, rephrasing sentences, carrying out written instruction, reacting emotionally to described events, and so on. Criterion-referenced tests seek to provide information regarding whether such kinds of performance can or cannot be demonstrated by an individual learner and not how much "reading ability" an examinee possesses along a hypothetical ability dimension. What is implied is some analysis of task structure in which each task description includes criteria of performance. This means that within a particular instructional context a test constructor is seldom free to choose at will the type of task he is to include in his test. This has been already delimited by definition of the domain of relevant tasks that describe the outcomes of learning. It also means that a scoring system must be devised that will preserve information about which tasks an individual can perform. Scores such as percentile ranks, stanines, and grade-equivalents preserve norm-group information but lose the specificity of criterion information.

A criterion-referenced test must also be generalizable to the task domain that the specific test tasks represent. One does not have to go very far in a curriculum sequence before the tasks that the learner is to perform become very large. To take a simple example, in an elementary arithmetic sequence, column addition appears relatively early. An instructionally relevant domain might consist of correct performance on all 3-, 4-, and 5-addend problems with the restriction that each addend be a single-digit integer from 0 through 9. The relevant domain of tasks consists of 111,000 addition problems. The measurement problem for criterion-referenced test constructors is how to build a test of reasonable length so that generalizations can be made about which specific problem types an individual learner can or cannot perform. Norm-referenced test constructors do not have such a problem since judicious selection of items will result in variable scores which spread out individuals, thus allowing one to say, "Johnny can do more than Suzy." The question of what Johnny can or cannot do is left unanswered. Yet, if instruction is to be adaptive to the individual learner, this information must be obtained. Is it problems which involve partial sums of a certain magnitude? Is it failure to apply the associative principle to simplify the calculation? These and many more such questions need to be answered in order to guide the instructional process.

The use to which achievement test information is put is another determinant of whether criterion-referenced or norm-referenced tests are needed. Both kinds of tests are used to make decisions about individuals, but the nature of the decisions determines the information required. In situations where there is a constraint on the number of individuals who can be admitted and in which some degree of selectivity is necessary, then comparisons among individuals are necessary and, hence, norm-referenced information is used. On the other hand, in educational situations where the requirement is to obtain information about the competencies possessed by a single individual before instruction can be provided, then criterion-referenced information is needed. Generally, in existing instructional systems that are relatively non-adaptive, admission decisions are made on a group basis and use norm-referenced data. As the feasibility of adaptive, individualized instruction increases, knowledge of an individual learner's position in the group becomes less important than knowledge of the competencies that the individual does or does not possess. Hence, it is likely that the requirements of educational measurement will be for criterion-referenced information in addition to norm-referenced information.

Finally, it is of interest to point out that the problem with which we are concerned was recognized over 50 years ago. In volume I of his *Educational Psychology*, E. L. Thorndike (1913) wrote the following:

ORIGINAL TENDENCIES AS ENDS: EMULATION IN THE
CASE OF SCHOOL "MARKS"

Present customs with respect to the measurement of a pupil's achievement in school studies fall into two groups. On the one hand, we have a somewhat detailed record kept, and made known to the student, in terms of a scale from 0 to 100, or from F through D−, D, D+, C−, C, C+, B−, B, B+, A− to A or A+. On the other hand, we have a deliberately crude record kept and made known to the student—such as F or P, or F, D, C, B, A. Or we have a crude or detailed record kept, but only some crude features of it made known to the student. During the last thirty years there has been a very strong movement from detailed to crude records of achievement, and from publicity to secrecy.

The reasons alleged for the change have been that detailed grades and publicity encourage a pupil to work for "marks," and for excellence in the sense of excelling others, instead of for knowledge or power, and for excellence in the sense of improvement.

In my opinion the change was an extremely wasteful way of avoiding one evil by the unnecessary sacrifice of all its attendant goods—a way whose wastefulness should have been apparent upon consideration of the nature of the situations involved and the original tendencies used. The essential fault of the older schemes for school grades or marks was that the "86" or "B−" did not mean any objectively defined amount of knowledge or power or skill—that, for example, John's attainment of 91 in second-year German did not inform him (or anyone else) about how difficult a passage he could translate, how many words he knew the English equivalents of and how accurately he could pronounce, or about any other fact save that he was supposed to be slightly more competent than someone else marked 89 was, or than he would have been if he had been so marked.

The marks given by any one teacher, though standing for some obscure standards of absolute achievement —that is, amounts of actual knowledge, power, skill, and the like—in the teacher's mind, could stand, in the mind of anyone else unacquainted with these meanings, only for degrees of relative achievement—for being at the top or at the bottom, for being above or below something. Inevitably other pupils were chosen as that something, and, except in the case of the one objectively defined difference between enough and not enough to allow promotion to the next class, school marks functioned as measures of superiority and inferiority amongst pupils, and of little else. A pupil who made excellence an aim of his school work was encouraged by every feature of the school's measurements of his work to think of excellence as *excelling others—relative achievement—outdoing someone else.* Finding that pupils did so, and being rightly suspicious of this gross form of emulation as an end in education, school officers took the easy, but wasteful, way of depriving the pupil of any save the vaguest knowledge of his achievement. To keep him from focussing his attention upon his achievement in comparison with his fellow students' achievements, they kept from him any detailed record whatsoever of his achievement.

To work for marks is not intrinsically bad. If the marks are, as they should be, correct measures of either the amount of knowledge, power, appreciation and skill attained or the amount of progress made, to work for marks means simply to work for knowledge, power, increase in knowledge and power and the like as recognized and measured. The detailed nature and the report to the individual of his school marks were not the vices of the old system. Its vice was its relativity and indefiniteness—the fact already described that a given mark did not mean any defined amount of knowledge, or power, or skill—so that it was bound to be used for relative achievement only.

The proper remedy is not to eliminate all stimulus to rivalry, and along with it a large part of the stimulus to achievement in general, but to redirect the rivalry into the tendencies to go higher on an objective scale for absolute achievement, to surpass one's own past performance, to get into what, in athletic parlance, is called a "higher class," to compete within that class, and to compete cooperatively as one of a group in rivalry with another group.

Suppose, for example, that instead of the traditional 89's or "good's," a pupil had records of just how many ten-digit additions he could compute correctly in five minutes, of just how difficult a passage he could translate correctly at sight, and of how long it required, and the like. He could, of course, still compare himself with others, but he would not be compelled to do so. He could be encouraged, instead, to compare his present achievement with last month's, to beat his record, or the record for an average ten-year-old, and to work for entrance to a "twenty-example" class comparable to the "two-thirty" class of trotting horses. In fact, in so far as excelling others would under these conditions imply and emphasize making absolute progress upward on a scale for real achievement, and would mean that a pupil outdid by a special effort those who ordinarily could do as well as he—those in his own "class" as that term is used in sport—even direct rivalry with others would be innocent and healthy.

Rivalry with one's own past and with a "bogey," or accepted standard, is entirely feasible, once we have absolute scales for educational achievement comparable to the scales for the speed at which one can run or the height to which one can jump. Such scales are being constructed. The strength of such impersonal rivalry as a motive, while not as great for the two or three who would compete to lead the class under the old system as that system's emphasis on rivalry with others, is far greater for the rest of the group. To be seventeenth instead of eighteenth, or twenty-third instead of twenty-fifth, does not approach in moving force the zeal to beat one's own record, to see one's practice curve rise week by week, and to get up to the standard which permits one to advance to a new feat.

The Applicability of
Criterion-Referenced
Measurement
by Content Area and Level

The Applicability of Criterion-Referenced Measurement by Content Area and Level

Alfred D. Garvin

University of Cincinnati

Certain writers are concerned today with *whether* we should use criterion-referenced measurement (CRM) or norm-referenced measurement (NRM); this essay deals with *when* each should be used. Although some writers clearly favor one above the other, their approaches suggest that, in any given case, there is a *choice* that could be made. I acknowledge that this grossly oversimplifies these writers' views. I will not oversimplify my own by stating merely that there never is a choice at all. The position that I take is this: In certain cases, CRM is irrelevant because, in fact, no meaningful criterion applies. In these cases, NRM must be used if there is to be any measurement at all. However, there are other cases where a meaningful criterion is inherent in the instructional objectives of the unit involved. If one measures the outcomes of such a unit at all, he is, in fact, conducting CRM. Between these two extremes, we might posit a continuum of relevance between criteria and instructional objectives.

The thesis I advance here may be summarized as follows: Our primary concern is with measuring the attainment of instructional objectives. The relevance of meaningful criteria to these instructional objectives dictates both the possibility of, and the necessity for, CRM. The relevance of criteria to instructional objectives is inherent in the content (and the level) of the instructional unit involved. Thus, for any given unit of instruction, we are not free to choose between CRM and NRM.

The basic issue that emerges here is, of course, the tenability of this thesis. In order to defend it, I will need a running start. I want to say some very fundamental things about instructional objectives, criteria, and measurement, *per se*, before presuming to prescribe the measurement technique to use for any given unit of instruction.

First of all, measurement is not an end in itself; we do not conduct instruction just to measure its effect.

Furthermore, the process of instruction is not an end in itself; the process is intended to accomplish something. A classical behaviorist might say that the general objective of all instruction is to change the *a priori* probabilities among response alternatives in an anticipatible situation. A hard-nosed pragmatist might say that the objective of instruction is to get something done—and done right! I offer this account: The objective of instruction is to cause a change in some modifiable trait within the individual instructed. The trait involved may be his knowledge of certain facts of U.S. history, his understanding of Boyle's law in physics, or his ability to translate selected passages from German into English. It may be his attitude toward all ethnic minorities, his belief in reincarnation, or his taste in literature. It may be his skill in parking trucks, playing tennis, or pulling teeth. If we add a psychomotor domain to the better-known cognitive and affective domains, we substantially anticipate most of the traits commonly specified in our instructional objectives.

Some of these traits are modifiable in degree; it is meaningful to speak of one having more or less of it and, by the conventions of trait-naming, having more of it is generally considered to be better than having less of it. Other traits are modifiable only in kind; changes in these traits are qualitative rather than quantitative. Most of these are comprehended in the affective domain of instructional objectives. While these may be as important as the quantitative traits, I will defer consideration of them here. A statement of instructional objectives must specify the desired final state of the trait or traits involved within the individual instructed. This may be the maximum level of which he is capable or it may be desired that he attain some predetermined level of this trait.

The necessity for any form of measurement at all arises in the fact that, ultimately, someone is going to *do* something about the extent to which different individuals attained these instructional objectives. This someone, or another someone, may also want to do something about the instructional process itself and/or those who conduct it. The primary purpose of measurement is to inform the decisions these somebodies must make.

There are two ways to measure the final state of any trait of interest in a group—and these two ways apply to any quantitative variable. We can compare the trait-levels attained by two or more individuals with each other or we can compare each such level with some "standard level." The first of these procedures is an operational definition of NRM; the second, of CRM. As a practical matter, it must be recognized that these traits are merely psychological constructs; to the extent that they have any being at all, they exist in the neural organization of the individual. The point is that they cannot be measured directly. What we do, of course, is this: We contrive a set of tasks (i.e., test items) that we judge to be valid behavioral correlates of the trait of interest. Next, we either rate performances on this set of tasks or simply count "successes" on some arbitrary basis. Then we take the score resulting from this process as a "measure" of this underlying trait. As we all know full well, this is easier to do for some traits than for others. Nevertheless, whether we are using NRM or CRM, we contrive a set of tasks that embody, in behavioral terms, the instructional objectives of the unit.

To the extent that these contrived classroom tasks correspond to some subsequent, extra-classroom task that must be performed at some "standard," i.e., criterion, level of proficiency in at least some situations, CRM is possible. Of course, this does not mean that it is desirable nor that it is feasible. We may turn now to a consideration of those extra-classroom tasks that might provide a "meaningful criterion" for our classroom tests.

There are certain tasks that, by their very nature, must be performed at a specifiably high level in almost every imaginable situation. Landing an airliner at O'Hare field is one; compounding a prescription is another. Any task in which public safety is involved falls in this category. There are other tasks in which some latitude of competence is permissible, even though a "criterion" level could be specified. No one would be seriously hurt if these were done less than perfectly and, in general, a deficient performance could be remedied. Cooking, housepainting, translating Latin, balancing checkbooks, and spelling fall in this category. There are tasks in which several different levels of performance are acceptable in as many different situations. There is a market for several different typing speeds, and one might translate foreign documents in minutes or in days. There are some tasks that need not be done to *any* standard. There is room in this world for third-rate poets, inept actors, and simply awful golfers. All of these abilities are acquired through instruction. To the extent that a "predetermined," i.e., criterion, level of performance in these tasks is crucial, the tests on such instruction ought to be criterion-referenced.

There is a class of instructional objectives in which the extra-classroom task envisioned is to be performed in the next classroom. Many units of instruction are intended primarily to prepare the individual to undertake the next unit in the sequence. To the extent that it is reasonable to specify an entering level of competence for this next unit, this level is a meaningful criterion for the present unit, whether or not the next unit is, itself, criterion-oriented. This is true in any cumulative content area. Mathematics and foreign languages are excellent examples.

There are two more things that must be said about "standards" or criteria—they arise from tasks performed *outside* the classroom, but they are *not independent* of the capabilities displayed within the classroom. An arbitrary standard of performance specified by the instructor is not a criterion, as I use the term. For purposes of his own, he may require that his students diagram four out of five selected sentences correctly or recite all the capitals of Europe in alphabetical order in one minute. These are not meaningful criteria. Requiring a correct diagnosis from a standard set of symptoms is. Next, a meaningful criterion must lie within the range of capabilities of those available to perform the task involved. It is pointless to demand prodigious reading speed for entry into third grade or to rate all piano students against a Horowitz recording. As a practical matter, criteria evolve from performance data gathered by NRM. The "predetermined" levels of performance the "real-world" requires in its important tasks are predetermined by available competence.

Before suggesting some general rules for matching measurement techniques with content areas and levels thereof, it would be well to reflect on the ultimate purpose of measurement—to inform decision making. Decisions must be made about individuals, and decisions must be made about tasks. If we must select a fixed quota from, say, the top of some available distribution of relevant ability, no matter how high or low this "top" level may be, NRM is indicated. If we must select individuals to perform a given task at some fixed standard of competence, no matter how many or how few qualify, then CRM is indicated. As previously explained, standards tend to accommodate available quotas, and the important work of the world does get done with the kinds of people there are.

When we apply the rationale developed above to the entire range of activities subsumed in the term "instruction," some general principles emerge regarding the applicability of CRM to various content areas and the various levels of these.

1. Unless at least one of the instructional objectives of a unit envisions a task that must subsequently be performed at a specified level of competence in at least some situation, CRM is irrelevant because there *is no* criterion. In this sense, the entire sequence of "social studies" provides no meaningful criterion except, possibly, the entry level for certain "honors" courses.

2. If public safety, economic responsibility, or other ethical considerations demand that certain tasks be performed only by those "qualified" for them by formal instruction, then CRM of the outcomes of such instruction is clearly indicated. The criterion here is the licensing standards of the profession involved. All professional instruction in the medical arts, law, finance, engineering, and the applied physical and social sciences generally is clearly in this category. Teaching—at any level—ought to be. However, entry to such professional training is typically based on NRM since training capacity imposes a "quota."

3. In any instructional sequence where the content is inherently cumulative and the rigor progressively greater, CRM should be used to control entry to successive units. However, if there are several different sequences, differing widely in rigor, NRM is more useful in making appropriate placements. The best examples of these are mathe-

matics and the physical and biological sciences in secondary school. Reading is the definitive example in the elementary grades.

4. There are certain content areas to which criteria *do* apply but not everyone need meet them. These are the "required subjects"; everyone must try to learn them—if only as a matter of public policy—but it is almost preordained that some of them will not. Home economics and physical education are relatively non-controversial examples at the secondary level; at the college level, these become professions and CRM applies.

At the outset of this paper, I said it would raise issues. I may live to regret it, but I must raise just one more. According to my rationale, English is a subject that not everyone need master. If my thesis can survive this outrageous implication, it can survive anything.

Evaluative Aspects of Criterion-Referenced Measures

Evaluative Aspects of Criterion-Referenced Measures

Richard C. Cox

University of Pittsburgh

While suggestions for criterion-referenced measurement have been available for some time, it has been only in the past few years that the notion has been pursued with interest. Unfortunately, the suggested usages reflect only a quite narrow definition of criterion-referenced measurement, when actually there are many ways in which the concept can provide meaningful test results. What is needed is a broader definition of the term, which will be accepted and used by more people in the educational measurement field. If this acceptance is to be forthcoming, there needs to be a re-examination of some of the evaluative aspects of measurement, such as reliability, validity, and item analysis procedures. Traditional approaches to these concepts may not be easily adaptable to criterion-referenced measurement; therefore, suggestions for gathering evaluative data should be explored.

The major distinction between norm-referenced and criterion-referenced measurement concerns the type of information provided. If, for example, an achievement test is administered in order to provide information about the performance of a pupil compared with that of other pupils, the measurement is said to be norm-referenced. Pupils are ordered with respect to each other or to some well defined norm group. While it is also possible to order pupils using criterion-referenced measurement, the more valuable information to result in this case is each pupil's performance relative to some specific standard. The essence of criterion-referenced measurement is in the specificity of information yielded in terms of pupil performance relative to some criterion. The following example illustrates this distinction between norm- and criterion-referenced measurement.

A graduate measurement examination is constructed to test the concepts of reliability, validity, and item analysis. After the test is administered, the scores can be interpreted in either a norm- or a criterion-referenced sense. If the instructor wishes to assign grades to individuals on the basis of the results, he may use the class as its own norm group and assign A's to those pupils with scores at least one standard deviation above the mean of the group, C's to those scoring at least one standard below the mean, with B's for the remaining scores. The grading could also be based upon certain percentile points, stanine scores, or other standard scores. Other appropriate norm groups may also be used, for example, the previous class. What is important in the measurement procedure is that the performance of individuals is compared with reference to some norm.

On the other hand, the test may be interpreted in a criterion-referenced manner. It may be the case that the instructor has established a criterion level of performance (such as 80 percent of all items answered correctly within each area) as an acceptable minimum standard. Pupils achieving this criterion performance are considered ready to study further measurement topics. Pupils who have not achieved the minimum standard may be given some form of remedial work or may just be considered as not having met the requirements. The important point here is that some specified performance level is the criterion and that the instructor is able to determine just what each pupil does or does not know in reference to each topic tested.

This example illustrates another often neglected point. It is possible for a single test to yield both norm-referenced and criterion-referenced information. (In fact, it has been suggested in an earlier paper that with certain adaptations, criterion-referenced data can be obtained from a typical standardized achievement test which has been designed to yield only norm-referenced information.) This is illustrative of the notion that criterion-referenced measurement need not be operationally defined in *such* a restricted sense.

Most available examples of criterion-referencing have been associated with individualized instructional programs. Coulson and Cogswell (1965) discuss the need for criterion-referencing in regard to the use of programmed materials utilized in individualized instructional systems. Glaser and Cox (1968) also suggest the use of criterion-referenced measures in individualized instruction models where the evaluation instruments must differentiate between groups of pupils who have mastered certain units of instruction and those who have not. While much of the impetus behind the discussion of criterion-referenced measurement has come from innovative instructional programs requiring precise specifications of instructional objectives, it would be unfortunate if this restricts further exploration of the concept.

Another restriction, recently discussed by Popham and Husek (1969), is that some of the traditional approaches to measurement theory are either not applicable or are difficult to adapt to the criterion-referenced framework. If the idea of criterion-referencing is to be accepted and used in educational measurement, there needs to be discussion and suggestions for some alternatives to reliability, validity, and item analysis procedures. The following discussion presents some suggestions for some new approaches to these concepts.

When an achievement test is constructed as a norm-referenced measure, the test items are written or selected to maximize differences between individuals. Maximum discrimination is desirable to obtain the variability necessary for ranking individuals. Similarly, most of the empirical methods for reporting reliability or validity indices require that the range of scores not be greatly restricted. Those test items which are answered correctly by all examinees or by no examinee will have difficulty levels of 1.00 and 0.00 respectively, and cannot discriminate in the usual sense between those scoring high and low on the total test. Items with characteristics like these will not contribute to test variance and will therefore be eliminated from a test designed to discriminate between individuals since their only effect is to add or subtract a constant value to or from every score.

A study by Cox and Vargas (1966) provides some data relevant to this point. Two discrimination indices were computed for items on tests which had been administered both as pre- and post-tests. The question of interest was the extent to which the two methods of item analysis yield the same relative evaluation of items. One index was computed using the common upper minus lower groups technique, thus providing information on how well each item discriminated between the groups. The second index involved both the pre- and post-test and was computed by subtracting the percentage of pupils who passed the item on the pre-test, from the percentage who passed the item on the post-test. This index provided discrimination information between pre- and post-test groups, indicating items useful for pre-test diagnosis. Results of the comparison between the two indices indicated that some items which are highly desirable for the pre-post test discrimination would be discarded by the typical item selection techniques, because they fail to discriminate among individuals taking the test. It was concluded that the pre- and post-test method of the item analysis produced results sufficiently different from traditional methods to warrant its consideration in those cases where score variability is not the concern, such as in criterion-referenced measures.

While this study proposed an approach to item analysis for criterion-referenced measures, it has application only in the pre-post test situation. There is certainly a need for some development work on item analysis procedures when only one test administration is possible. Considerations like these must be given attention if the criterion-referenced concept is to be broadened.

Exactly what happens to the concepts of validity and reliability when applied to criterion-referenced measures is not clear. It may be the case that the usual coefficients are adequate; it is also quite possible that the criterion-referenced measure will not yield sufficient variability to make these typical coefficients meaningful. Consider, for example, the case where all individuals taking the test answer all of the items correctly. Not only will the items have no discriminating power among individuals, but also due to the absence of variance it may not be possible to interpret traditional reliability or validity coefficients.

A study by Cox and Graham (1966) illustrates one way in which reliability may be viewed, given a special type of criterion-referenced measure. They described the development of a sequentially scaled achievement test designed for use in an instructional system within which certain performance objectives can be identified as being sequential in nature. Theoretically, in this situation it seems possible to construct a test in such a way that the pupil answers all items up to a certain point (his level of attainment) and misses all items beyond that point. The test would be scaled in the Guttman sense, the total test score indicating the response pattern of the individual. (This is a good example of criterion-referenced measurement where the test information is quite specific with reference to examinee performance according to some criteria.) The analysis of a group of such scores yields a coefficient of reproducibility which indicates how well an individual's response pattern can be reproduced from a knowledge of his total score. This coefficient, while usually considered as a verification of the arrangement of items, might also be used as a type of reliability estimate across all individuals taking the test. The pitfalls of using reproducibility as a reliability estimate for achievement tests has not yet been explored.

Validity is a major concern in criterion-referenced measurement. The emphasis on obtaining information specific to pupil performance with reference to some criterion makes obvious the need for validity. As always, these validity estimates must be determined by the purpose for which the test is being used. Certain uses will dictate certain necessary validities. In general, however, criterion-referencing itself suggests that validity must depend upon the correspondence of the test items with the objectives to which the test is referenced. Criterion-referenced tests, then, must provide information in terms of specific behavior. Thus the test items must be constructed for, or matched to, goals of instruction. The desired measurement must provide information in terms of pupil performance relative to some criterion and therefore demands a rigorous validation procedure.

The use of experimental techniques to establish the validity of a criterion-referenced measure should be investigated (i. e., construct-validation procedures). An example might be that if teaching techniques have been effective, then a pupil who has worked through a given unit of content should attain a higher score on a post-test than a pupil who has not yet been exposed to the unit content. Many such operational definitions could be examined under the heading of construct validity.

In summary, the plea has been made to interpret the

concept of criterion-referenced measurement in a broader sense, so that the idea will be utilized in more ways in educational measurement. While applications of the concept have been suggested mainly for programs of individualization, there is no reason to limit the ideas of criterion-referenced measurement to such application. There needs to be some thought given to how the criterion-referenced concept can be applied to the typical teacher-made test as well as to standardized tests. Also, if the idea is to be accepted, some alternative to the traditional approaches to reliability, validity, and item analysis procedures must be investigated.

References

Coulson, J. E. and Cogswell, J. F. Effects of individualized instruction on testing. *Journal of Educational Measurement, 2* (1), 59-64, 1965.

Cox, R. C. and Graham, G. T. The development of a sequentially scaled achievement test. *Journal of Educational Measurement, 3* (2), 147-150, 1966.

Cox, R. C. and Vargas, J. S. A comparison of item selection techniques for norm-referenced and criterion-referenced tests. Paper read at the annual meeting of the National Council on Measurement in Education, Chicago, Illinois, February 1966.

Glaser, R. and Cox, R. C. Criterion-referenced testing for the measurement of educational outcomes. In R. A. Weisgerber (editor), *Instructional process and media innovation.* Chicago, Illinois: Rand-McNally and Co., 1968, pp. 545-550.

Popham, W. J. and Husek, T. R. Implications of criterion-referenced measurement. *Journal of Educational Measurement, 6,* (1), 1-9, 1969.

Indices of Adequacy for Criterion-Referenced Test Items

Indices of Adequacy for Criterion-Referenced Test Items

W. James Popham

University of California, Los Angeles

A considerable amount of attention has recently been given to the properties of criterion-referenced measures in contrast to more traditional norm-referenced approaches. This attention has extended beyond the ethereal realms of the psychometric journals, even penetrating

The writing of this paper was partially supported by the Division of Comprehensive and Vocational Education Research, United States Office of Education, Department of Health, Education, and Welfare. The opinions expressed herein, however, do not necessarily represent the position or policy of the U.S. Office of Education, and no official endorsement by the U.S. Office of Education should be inferred.

the day-to-day decision making world of public school personnel. But while the number of textbooks and expository articles regarding norm-referenced testing could be stacked in a fairly respectable pile (size, not quality), there are few guides available to the constructor of criterion-referenced tests. In part, this deficiency exists because few measurement specialists have yet directed their efforts toward writing practitioners' handbooks for criterion-referenced test construction. Beyond that, however, we currently don't have a collection of handy maxims for such test construction. While well-honed notions such as discrimination indices and internal consistency estimates abound in the norm-referenced arena, few such procedures are now available to the person who must generate and refine criterion-referenced measures.

This paper will recount some frustrations in an attempt to identify useful indicators by which a criterion-referenced item writer could judge the adequacy of his test items. The effort to locate such indicators resulted from (1) program assessment efforts at the Southwest Regional Laboratory for Educational Research and Development (SWRL) where for many months an intermittent but persistent dialogue among staff members has taken place regarding these questions and (2) investigations in the UCLA Center for the Study of Evaluation, particularly those associated with PROBE (Project for Research on Objectives Based Evaluation), a major activity of the Center.

The quest of a criterion-referenced item writer should be for his test items to accurately sample the range of criterion behavior which they are designed to measure. In a typical instructional situation, this means that test items should possess congruency with the class of eligible behaviors circumscribed by an instructional objective.

An A Priori *Approach*

Currently, the most useful scheme for writing items which possess congruency with a criterion has been provided by Hively and his associates (Hively, W., 1970) in their work on *domain-referenced achievement testing*. In this system an *item form* constitutes a complete set of rules for generating a domain of test items which can be used to accurately measure a particular objective.

Particularly in fields such as mathematics, the use of well explicated limits, similar to those employed in the item form approach, prove most useful. Independent judges tend to agree on whether a given test item is congruent with the highly specific behavior domain explicated by the item form. For example, it is readily apparent whether addition problems do, in fact, only possess double digit numbers as dictated by the generation rules, in an item form. As one moves to somewhat less well defined fields, however, the fog thickens. It is far more difficult to prepare item forms so that they yield test items which can be subsequently judged congruent with a given instructional objective. Either the item form becomes so lengthy it is cumbersome to use, or dissimilar interpretations of appropriate items may emerge.

Perhaps the best approach to developing adequate criterion-referenced test items will be to sharpen our skill in developing item forms which are parsimonious but also permit the production of high congruency test items.

A Posteriori *Approaches*

An alternative attack on this problem may be to develop the test items with whatever generation rules are available, then try the items out to discover empirically which items are defective, that is, are not congruent with the criterion. A better way to put it might be to say that we wish to discover defective item forms, namely, those which permit the generation of incongruous items.

In an attempt to devise some indicators of item adequacy (or item form adequacy) on the basis of empirical tryout data, two sets of test items and data resulting from their use were scrutinized at some length. The first was a group of criterion-referenced test items developed to assess the effectiveness of a SWRL instructional program. The second was a collection of test items used in an instructional methodology class at UCLA. The remainder of this paper will report the data, some analyses, and some speculations regarding both of these sets of items.

Instructional Concepts Program Test Items

The first test items used were constructed to assess the

effectiveness of the SWRL Instructional Concepts Program, a sequence designed to teach preschool children certain conceptual skills required in academic tasks. The rationale and effectiveness of the program are described elsewhere (Scott, 1969).

In all, there were 35 test items representing seven different program objectives, five items per objective. Each item consisted of a flashcard coupled with oral directions. The flashcard contained one illustration of the concept being tested and either one or two distractors. A child would be told "Point to the green bird," and was then obliged to select the correct illustration. With the exception of four two-choice items, all items were of a three-choice form.

These items were administered on a pre- and post-instruction basis to 133 kindergarten children from low income San Diego and Santa Paula families during 1968-1969. A 15-week instructional program was under analysis, and the identical items were given as a pretest and posttest. From these 133 children, 100 were randomly selected for ease of interpretation. Their pretest and posttest data were subjected to several analyses. In each case the five-item subtests were considered separately, that is, as distinct tests of five items apiece.

Replicating the Cox-Vargas Analysis

An initial analysis was conducted in the same fashion as Cox and Vargas (1966) in their attempt to contrast classical norm-referenced item analysis approaches with a procedure more consistent with criterion-referenced consideration. They ranked sets of test items according to two different indices, then computed the correlation between these two sets of rankings. Their *Difference Index* was computed on posttest data only, as is typically the case with norm-referenced approaches, by calculating "the percentage of students in the highest 27 per cent in total posttest score who pass the item minus the percentage in the lowest 27 per cent who pass the item." Their *Pretest-Posttest Difference Index* was obtained by computing "the percentage of students who pass the item on the posttest minus the percentage who pass the item on the pretest." For two different sets of items, addition and multiplication, the correlation coefficients between the two different ranking approaches were .37 and .40 respectively.

For the seven different subtests of the Instruction Concepts Program items, the correlations between the same two ranking approaches were as follows: .70, .63, 1.00, 0, 0, .34, .90. The zero coefficients resulted from tied ranks on the five-item subsets.

A Fourfold Fantasy

Another approach that seemed promising for criterion-referenced tests used in association with an instructional sequence was to consider the particular changes which occurred with items over the 15-week instructional period.

Four possibilities exist. For any learner an item could be answered incorrectly (0) on the pretest, then correctly (1) on the posttest, and thus be designated for that individual as a 01 item. Similarly 00, 11, or 10 responses could occur. The possible results of each of the 100 individuals completing the pretest and posttest can be represented as in Figure 1. Cell A can be thought of as the positive change cell while Cell D represents the negative change cell.

		Posttest	
		Correct	Incorrect
Incorrect		01	00
		(A)	(B)
Pretest			
Correct		11	10
		(C)	(D)

Figure 1.
A Fourfold Table Representing Possible Pretest-Posttest
Performance on Test Items

For each of the items the percentages of individuals responding in each of these four ways were calculated. Next, items were ranked according to the highest percentage of responses in first the 01, then the 10 categories. Where overall improvement during instruction is present, as was the case with all seven subtests, the 01 category (Cell A) would seem to be tapping this improvement, while the 10 category (Cell D) would not seem to be reflecting it. A negative correlation between the two sets of rankings was anticipated. As can be seen in Table 1 where these data are presented, such a negative relationship was not present. Indeed, the coefficients on the seven subtests between the 01 and 10 rankings were as follows: -.10, .87, .82, 1.00, -.10, .97, -.10.

Homogeneity

Another way of analyzing the fourfold data might be to locate items which behaved aberrantly, at least with respect to most other items in a subtest. Because a common approach to the detection of such aberrance, namely, intercorrelation among test items, often fails with criterion-referenced tests because of insufficient variability in post-instruction test performance, a chi square analysis seemed to be a likely alternative. For each of the subtests of five items, a four by five chi square analysis could reveal the degree to which the items congealed with respect to the four options, i.e., 00, 01, 10, 11. Where significant chi square values resulted, the aberrant item(s) could be more closely scrutinized.

Unfortunately, for these seven subtests six whopping chi square values emerged, suggesting a probable lack of utility for this approach. For the seven subtests (with 12 *df*) the respective chi square results were 15.5, 192.3,

109.3, 180.1, 49.8, 257.2 and 35.6. A chi square of 26.2 is required for .01 significance in this situation.

Other Fun

Several alternative methods of ranking the test items within subsets were tried, 13 in all. Intercorrelations among all of them were computed for each of the seven subtests (making a thicker than comfortably carried computer printout). Some of these ranking procedures proved to be redundant, correlating perfectly with others. Some proved slightly, but not meaningfully, different from the four ranking schemes previously described, i.e., Cox and Vargas' two procedures plus the 01 and 10 procedures. For example, rankings based on (1) a McNemar significance of change statistic and (2) a phi coefficient on the fourfold data did not yield any readily interpretable results. Some of the 13 ranking procedures were calculated only because the computer had been taught to dispense them.

Instructional Methodology Class Test Items

The second set of data was based upon four ten-item subtests used in a UCLA course for secondary teacher education candidates. Each of these subtests dealt with a particular facet of the topic of instructional objectives. Subtest I required students to distinguish between measurable and nonmeasurable instructional objectives. Subtest II required discriminations between objectives which did or did not possess a minimum level of acceptable performance for an individual learner. Subtest III called for discriminations between objectives which did or did not possess a minimum level of acceptable performance for a group of learners. Subtest IV presented a series of objectives which were to be classified according to the taxonomy of educational objectives as primarily (a) affective, (b) psychomotor, (c) cognitive-lowest level, or (d) cognitive-higher than lowest level. Thus, Subtests I, II, and III consisted of binary choice items while Subtest IV was composed of four alternative multiple choice items.

The four subtests were administered as part of a pretest at the beginning of a UCLA course during the fall, 1969 quarter, again as a part of the midterm examination in the course five weeks later, and as a part of the final examination in the course still five weeks later. The principal instruction regarding these four topics occurred prior to the midterm exam, but the topics were also treated intermittently after the midterm examination. Almost 200 students were enrolled in the class. Once more, for ease of interpretation, 100 students' examinations were selected at random for use in all analyses.

Essentially, both the midterm and final examination performance of the subjects can be considered posttests. Both were used since it was anticipated that while student performance on the midterm examination would be high, there would be an even higher performance, hence less

Table 1.

Frequency distribution of correct (1) and incorrect (0) responses for pretest-posttest performance of 100 subjects based on the SWRL Instructional Concepts Program.

Pretest-Posttest Frequencies

Subtest	Item	01	00	11	10
	1	8	3	88	1
	2	15	3	82	0
I	3	11	1	85	3
	4	14	0	85	1
	5	21	2	75	2
	6	18	1	77	4
	7	25	51	16	8
II	8	36	11	47	6
	9	14	2	80	4
	10	44	20	27	9
	11	17	5	71	7
	12	16	11	72	1
III	13	33	16	33	18
	14	7	3	89	1
	15	11	1	86	2
	16	16	4	75	5
	17	12	1	87	0
IV	18	13	9	74	4
	19	31	45	11	13
	20	22	27	39	12

(Continued next page)

Table 1 continued:

Pretest-Posttest Frequencies

Subject	Item	01	00	11	10
	21	22	23	34	21
	22	35	9	52	4
V	23	27	15	53	5
	24	30	12	54	4
	25	23	28	40	9
	26	11	2	85	2
	27	7	0	92	1
VI	28	26	25	38	11
	29	31	36	23	10
	30	24	61	6	9
	31	12	6	76	6
	32	16	8	68	8
VII	33	27	15	55	3
	34	18	7	71	4
	35	33	16	45	6

variability, on the final examination. Both situations were of interest. Thus, during the remainder of this discussion these two posttests will be referred to as the "midterm posttest" and the "final posttest."

Cox-Vargas Replication

For each of the four subtests the ten items were ranked on the basis of Cox-Vargas' Difference Index and their Pretest-Posttest Difference Index. These rankings were then correlated. Results for both posttests are presented in Table 2.

Table 2.

Correlations between Cox-Vargas' Difference Index and Pretest-Posttest Difference Index for 100 subjects' performance on four ten-item instructional methodology subtests.

	Midterm Posttest	Final Posttest
Subtest	r^*	r^*
I	$-.37$	$-.34$
II	$-.03$	$-.18$
III	$-.23$	$-.02$
IV	$-.33$	$.17$

*An r of .55 or more is required for .05 significance.

While none of the resulting correlations attained the strength necessary for statistical significance, it is clear from these results, as well as those of the Instructional Concepts Program data, that the two indices yield markedly disparate information regarding the adequacy of test items, particularly where the level of posttest proficiency is high.

Fourfold Results

Employing the same four-cell tabulation scheme as was described earlier, the data were arrayed as seen in Table 3.

Table 3

Frequency distribution of correct (1) and incorrect (0) responses for pretest-posttest performance of 100 subjects on four subtests based on a UCLA instructional methodology course.

Subtest	Item	Midterm Posttest				Final Posttest			
		01	00	11	10	01	00	11	10
	1	20	0	80	0	20	0	80	0
	2	25	1	69	5	26	0	72	2
	3	20	0	76	0	20	0	79	1
	4	22	0	78	0	22	0	78	0
I	5	14	1	83	2	15	0	81	4
	6	12	0	88	0	12	0	88	0
	7	30	0	70	0	30	0	70	0
	8	27	0	72	1	27	0	73	0
	9	24	0	76	0	24	0	76	0
	10	16	0	82	2	16	0	84	0
	1	23	1	76	0	24	0	76	0
	2	34	10	43	8	31	13	40	16
	3	27	38	22	13	39	26	20	15
	4	57	19	16	8	73	3	22	2
II	5	39	0	61	0	39	0	61	0
	6	16	0	82	2	16	0	81	3
	7	19	8	52	21	24	3	62	11
	8	36	8	53	3	37	7	43	13
	9	17	0	82	1	16	1	83	0
	10	11	3	84	2	14	0	85	1

(Continued next page)

Table 3 continued:

Subtest	Item	Midterm Posttest				Final Posttest			
		01	00	11	10	01	00	11	10
	1	29	1	70	0	28	2	69	1
	2	51	5	42	2	55	1	42	2
	3	42	14	33	11	48	8	38	6
	4	38	1	59	2	36	3	58	3
III	5	42	6	47	5	42	6	42	10
	6	35	6	50	9	38	3	57	2
	7	43	22	28	7	51	14	28	7
	8	37	4	54	5	36	5	55	4
	9	39	2	59	0	39	2	57	2
	10	24	4	66	6	24	4	65	7
	1	50	0	50	0	50	0	50	0
	2	62	4	33	1	65	1	30	4
	3	69	0	31	0	69	0	30	1
	4	43	2	54	1	45	0	55	0
IV	5	48	3	47	2	50	1	49	0
	6	69	2	28	1	65	6	29	0
	7	42	21	23	14	24	39	27	10
	8	56	2	40	2	58	0	41	1
	9	64	4	31	1	64	4	32	0
	10	63	5	29	3	66	2	29	3

Once more, correlations were computed between rankings based on frequencies in the negative change cell and positive change cell. Unsystematic correlation coefficients emerged, as can be seen in Table 4.

Table 4

Correlations between rankings based on 01 and 10 frequencies for the instructional methodology class test results.

	Midterm Posttest	Final Posttest
Subtest	r^*	r^*
I	−.07	−.19
II	.13	.27
III	.08	.15
IV	−.44	.16

*An r of .55 or more is required for .05 significance.

Homogeneity

As with the Instructional Concepts Program data, chi square analyses were computed on the eight four by ten tables representing both posttest results for the four subtests. The resulting eight chi square values were Subtest I: 48.3 and 40.5; Subtest II: 376.4 and 371.5; Subtest III: 133.3 and 96.7; Subtest IV: 183.4 and 350.6. Since a chi square value of 40 is required for .05 significance, it can be seen that all eight values proved to be statistically significant. Since with Subtest I, both regarding the midterm and final exams, the chi square values failed to achieve .01 significance, perhaps the use of this type of analysis with a stringent level of significance may prove of some utility as a gross test of the homogeneity of a set of supposedly similar test items.

Further Fumbling

Once more, a number of different schemes for ranking the test items in each set were computed and correlated with each other, as well as the several variations available from the fourfold data, e.g., the 01 and 10 frequencies. Nothing resonated.

But from this confusion one insight emerged, namely, the quest was for a readily computed red flag which, much as a negative discrimination index for a norm-referenced test item, alerts the test constructor to a potentially deficient item. Now one could argue that such items are identifiable by simple inspection of the fourfold frequencies for a set of items administered on a pre- and post-instruction basis. For instance, in situations where there is some positive change attributable to instruction, as reflected by fairly consistent pretest to posttest improvement,[1] then one might scrutinize data such as those in Table 3 to detect items which were behaving aberrantly. For instance, if one examines the midterm posttest results for Subtest II, then certainly items no. 3 and no. 7 seem to be measuring something different from most

1. It should be emphasized that general pre- to post-instruction improvement must be occurring for this type of homogeneity analysis to make sense. Otherwise, many items which are behaving chaotically may merely be reflective of poor instruction.

of the other items in that set. In Subtest I, on the other hand, there appear to be no particularly aberrant items. But, visual scrutiny carries with it the dangers of misperception on the part of the scrutinizer. It would be pleasant to have some easily calculated, yet reliable, index of item aberrance.

A Possibility?

After considerable thought, a possible solution emerged. What we really wish to do is locate the items that behave differently from most of the items or, putting it another way, behave differently from the *prototypic item*. But what is the prototypic item for a set of items ostensibly measuring the same objective? Perhaps the best estimate of such an item can be attained by computing the median values for the 01, 00, 11, and 10 cells of a four by k table such as the subsets of Table 3. The median value would not be affected by the aberrant items (as would the arithmetic mean), yet would provide some indication of how most of the items were behaving. By contrasting each item's actual fourfold frequencies with hypothetical frequencies based on the median values for each cell we arrive at a one by four cell table which permits a chi square test with three degrees of freedom.

Such chi square analyses were computed for each of the items in the four instructional methodology class subtests. The results are presented in Table 5. An inspection of the results does suggest the possible utility of this approach, for the particularly large chi square values do seem to pick up the atypical items, even more accurately than visual scrutiny.

Table 5

Chi square values yielded by contrasting fourfold frequencies of each item with hypothetical frequencies based on the median value of each ten-item subtest.

	Subtest I		Subtest II		Subtest III		Subtest IV	
Item	Mid	Final	Mid	Final	Mid	Final	Mid	Final
1	.8	.3	12.7	8.3	16.3	7.3	15.2	15.1
2	48.2	16.6	22.5	141.4	7.8	13.0	1.1	24.8
3	24.7	2.9	257.8	383.3	34.5	15.7	5.5	2.6
4	.7	.3	115.7	101.3	5.4	.4	19.6	24.3
5	13.4	68.7	16.1	9.3	1.3	17.7	9.6	12.9
6	6.1	5.2	19.8	13.1	4.1	.7	2.3	25.9
7	5.1	5.0	139.9	29.8	80.4	53.0	274.4	1647.5
8	2.7	2.3	6.4	65.4	.2	.9	2.7	4.9
9	1.1	.7	19.9	15.3	7.3	1.3	1.4	9.7
10	6.1	1.8	21.9	18.5	9.5	10.5	5.5	14.0

For example, the chi square values for the midterm data on Subtest II signalled that item no. 4 was behaving more aberrantly than our visual examination had detected. Incidentally, all three items in this subtest (nos. 3, 4, and 7) were subsequently discerned to have been badly written.

Exactly how to set the minimum limits for such chi square values is yet to be worked out, but when the value exceeds 1,000 with three degrees of freedom, as was the case for item no. 7 in Subtest IV Final Posttest, then a magenta flag is clearly fluttering. There are, of course, technical considerations in the calculations of such chi square tests, e.g., expected median frequencies of zero as would occur in the Final Subtest I for the 00 cell, which may result in other, comparable analyses being employed. What is being recommended here is not this particular analysis, but a general approach for producing an empirically-based index of defective criterion-referenced test items used to assess the quality of instruction.

References

Cox, Richard C. and Julie S. Vargas. A Comparison of Item Selection Techniques for Norm-Referenced and Criterion-Referenced Tests. Paper presented at the annual meeting of the National Council on Measurement in Education, Chicago, Illinois, February 1966.

Hively, Wells, II. Introduction to Domain-Referenced Achievement Testing. Symposium Presentation, American Educational Research Association, Minneapolis, Minnesota, March 2-6, 1970.

Scott, Roger O. The 1968-1969 Classroom Tryout of the SWRL Instructional Concepts Program. *SWRL Development Memorandum,* July 10, 1969. 22 pp.

Selected References

Selected References

Prepared by Leonard L. Streeter

Astin, Alexander W. Criterion-centered research. *Educational and Psychological Measurement*, 1964, 24:4, 807-822.

Berger, Robert J. Criterion-referenced testing with the SWRL communications program. Southwest Regional Laboratory Memorandum. Inglewood, California: Southwest Regional Laboratory, 1969.

Bloom, Benjamin S. Learning for mastery. *Evaluation Comment*, Center for the Study of Evaluation, 1968, 1:2.

Cartier, Francis A. Criterion-referenced testing of language skills. ERIC Microfilms, 1968, ED 020 515.

Coulson, J. E. and Cogswell, J. F. Effects of individualized instruction on testing. *Journal of Educational Measurement*, 2:1, 1965.

Cox, R. C. and Vargas, Julie S. A comparison of item

selection techniques for norm-referenced and criterion-referenced tests. ERIC Microfilms ED 010517, 1966.

Cronbach, L. J. Evaluation for course improvement. *Teachers College Record,* 1963, 65, 672-683.

Ebel, Robert L. Must all tests be valid? *American Psychologist,* 1961, 16, 640-647.

Ebel, Robert L. Content standard test scores. *Educational and Psychological Measurement,* 1962, 22, 15-25.

Ebel, Robert L. Some measurement problems in a national assessment of educational progress. *Journal of Educational Measurement,* 1966, 3:1, 11-17.

Ebel, Robert L. The value of internal consistency in classroom examinations. *Journal of Educational Measurement,* 1968, 5:1, 71-73.

Ebel, Robert L. Some limitations of criterion-referenced measurement. American Educational Research Association. ERIC Microfilms, 1970, ED 038 670.

Ferguson, Richard L. Computer assisted criterion-referenced testing. Working paper no. 49. Pittsburgh University, Pennsylvania. Learning Research and Development Center, ERIC Microfilms, 1969, ED 040 061.

Flanagan, J. Units, scores, and norms. *Educational Measurement.* (Ed.) E. F. Lindquist, American Council on Education, Washington, D. C., 1951, 695-763.

Glaser, R. and Klaus, D. J. Proficiency measurement: Assessing human performance. *Psychological Principles in System Development.* (Ed.) R. Gagne, New York, Holt, Rinehart & Winston, 1962, 421-427.

Glaser, R. and Cox, R. C. Criterion-referenced testing for the measurement of educational outcomes. *Instructional Process and Media Integration.* (Ed.) Robert Weisgerber, Rand-McNally, Chicago, 1967.

Halls, W. D. Analysis of aims and content as a basis for assessment of school courses. *Comparative Education,* 1969, 5:3, 213-220.

Horn, John L. Some characteristics of classroom examinations. *Journal of Educational Measurement,* 1966, 3:4, 293-295.

Horn, John L. Is it reasonable for assessments to have different psychometric properties than predictors? *Journal of Educational Measurement,* 1968, 5:1, 75-77.

Klein, Stephen. Evaluating tests in terms of the information they provide. Unpublished manuscript. Center for the Study of Evaluation, University of California at Los Angeles.

Kriewall, Thomas E. *Applications of information theory and acceptance sampling principles to the management of mathematics instruction.* Technical report no. 103, Wisconsin Research and Development Center for Cognitive Learning, The University of Wisconsin, 1969.

Livingston, Samuel A. The reliability of criterion-referenced measures. Paper prepared for an AERA Symposium. New York, N. Y., 1971.

Millman, Jason. Reporting student progress: A case for a criterion-referenced marking system. Working Papers in Educational Research, number 5, Cornell University, 1970.

Moxley, R. A. A source of disorder in the schools and a way to reduce it: two kinds of tests. *Teacher & Technology Supplement, Educational Technology,* March, 1970.

Shoemaker, D. M. Criterion-referenced measurement revisited. *Educational Technology,* March, 1971.

Simon, George B. Comments on "Implications of criterion-referenced measurement." *Journal of Educational Measurement,* 1969, 6:4, 259-260.

Skager, Rodney W. Objective based evaluation: Macro evaluation. American Educational Research Association, ERIC Microfilms, 1970, ED 038 710.

Trow, Wm. Clark *Paths to educational reform.* Englewood Cliffs, New Jersey: Educational Technology Publications, 1971.

Tucker, L. Scales minimizing the importance of referenced groups. In *Proceedings, Invitational Conference on Testing Problems.* Princeton, New Jersey: Educational Testing Service, 1952, 22-28.

Unks, Nancy J. An investigation of validity and reliability concepts for criterion-referenced measurement. Unpublished masters thesis, University of Pittsburgh, 1969.

Warrington, Willard G. Criterion related measures: Some general considerations. Paper prepared for the AERA Symposium, "Criterion Related Measurement: Bane or Boon?" Minneapolis, Minn., March, 1970.

The Authors

The Authors

Robert Glaser is director, Learning Research and Development Center, and professor of psychology and education, University of Pittsburgh. His major professional interests are in theory and experimentation in the psychology of instruction; the development of experimental school models for adapting to individual differences; basic studies on children's acquisition of complex behavior; and investigations of computer assistance to the elementary school.

W. James Popham is professor, Graduate School of Education, University of California, Los Angeles, and director of the Instructional Objectives Exchange at UCLA.

The late *T. R. Husek* was a member of the faculty at the University of California, Los Angeles.

Alfred D. Garvin is assistant professor of education and coordinator of graduate programs in educational research at the University of Cincinnati. He teaches graduate courses in research design, measurement, statistics, and computer applications. Current research interest is on affective factors in achievement testing and grading.

Richard C. Cox is director of the University of Pittsburgh's Office of Measurement and Evaluation, which provides test administration and scoring, and consulting services to the faculty and staff. He is associate professor of education in the Department of Educational Research at the University of Pittsburgh, teaching a course in measurement.